Introduction to Library and Information Science

By

Dr.Syed Shah Ahmed Sarmast
MA,MLISC.Ph.D

About Book

The book **"INTRODUCTION TO LIBRARY AND INFORMATION SCIENCE"** by Dr. Syed Shah Ahmed Sarmast is unique and blend of theory and practice with modern approach, the basic profession useful for UG, PG Students, Research Scholar and Teachers. The Library Automation and the Information Technology application chapter has made the treatise worth for Teaching and learning community. This book will prove assets to libraries.

Professor B.S Nigam,
Head Dept. of Library and Information Science,
MCRP, University, BHOPAL (M.P).

About Author

Dr. Syed Shah Ahmed Sarmast, has completed M.A (Sociology) from Gulbarga University, Gulbarga in 1995, MLISc (Library & Information Science)from Gulbarga University, Gulbarga in 1999. In 2008 MCRP University, Bhopal has awarded Ph.D in Library and Information Science in 2008. He served all fields of Library and Information Science. He has published more than 15 Articles in Library and Information Science in LIS Journals. He has written 4 books (include this book) he has attended and presented the papers in many National and International Seminars of Library and Information Science. He is also research guide in Mewar University, Rajasthan and Career Point University, Rajasthan in Library and Information Science.

Dr. Syed Shah Ahmed Sarmast

Table of Contents

chapter .1
Concept of library & Its Importance

Introduction

Libraries have been around for a very long time and are traditionally seen as collections of information and services. Libraries have always played an important role, enabling people to engage with all kinds of information and knowledge resources. Through, the technological development of electronic resources the means to collect, store, manage, and use widely distributed knowledge resources have become more effective serving the Library users even better). Modern libraries are therefore called as places to get wider access to information in many formats and from many sources.

The Technological development in libraries has affected both information space and information practice. Today we talk about libraries without walls being logical extensions to libraries. An important development in the second half of the 20th century was the introduction of integrated library systems and online catalogues giving access to information on library collections from anywhere with an internet connection. The idea of the library room changed when much of the visibility of the library environment was on the screen .The distance between author and reader has been shortened while it gives a more direct involvement in the dissemination of information. Libraries provide access to an endless variety of information resources and opportunities for interactive communication. However, the fundamental mission has remained, to facilitate and give access to information and knowledge, but the processes, tools, and techniques have undergone big development.

At the same time the fact that the web is accessible from every corner of the world has meant that users are presented the same interface which is found problematic while it is difficult to design an interface that suits such a wide range of users. Therefore the development has also included a shift towards personalization and initiatives like My Library have emerged. These are a further development of digital libraries, which define personalized library services to Web users who expect customization and interactivity. Surprisingly for developers of these services, the adoption rates of these services have been very low and therefore it is important to look deeper into the barriers to personalized service as this seems to be the future of the digital world. New trends concerning personalization, self service, and mobility have created a Web environment that is transforming how users are interacting with information. The user becomes a partner and a contributor to the work of the library which means the understanding of users becomes even more important.

Meaning & Definition

The English Term "Library" is derived from Latin word ' Liber,' means A "book." In Greek and the Romance languages, the corresponding term is bibliotheca. Means collection or group of collections of books and/or other print or non Book materials organized and maintained for use (reading, consultation, study, research, etc.).

OED defines Library as "A building or room containing collections of books, periodicals, and sometimes films and recorded music for use or borrowing by the public or the members of an institution." Wikipedia, the free encyclopedia (on line) defines "library is a collection of sources of information and similar resources, made accessible to a defined community for reference or borrowing.[1] It provides physical or digital access to material, and may be a physical building or room, or a virtual space, or both.[2]

Types of libraries

Library is the store-house of knowledge for posterior use. Human knowledge can be recorded and preserved in different media. Some years back, documents written or printed in paper were considered as the best medium. But with the development of science and technology today electronic multimedia have been widely used for preservation of knowledge in the libraries of any kind whether it may be public, academic, national or special library. Since the beginning of civilization human beings have been putting emphasis on storing of information in different ways. However it must be admitted that libraries in ancient times were not like those of the present days. Libraries are dynamic and grow along with human civilization. The urge of social, economic, intellectual and cultural improvement necessitates the development of different kinds of libraries.

Since knowledge and information are so vital for all round development, libraries that handle and manage knowledge and information are invaluable indeed. The present knowledge society has been, as understood, characterized by the competition, the supply and demand for knowledge to meet the varied and complex needs of the individuals, which are expected from the library. Dissemination of right information to the right reader /user at the right time is the dictum of all the library and information centers. In short library is an agency for dissemination of information. The basic function of library is education. The purpose of a library in modern society is to educate the community in a wider sense. Libraries play a very important role in the educational process of formal and non-formal learning, in research and development, in cultural activities, in spiritual and ideological realms, in recreation and entertainment etc. With the spectacular advances in information technology and increasing categories of users and their information needs in different situations, modern society is heading towards an information society in which the central instrument of change, force and direction of change are knowledge and information. According to the mode of services rendered to the readers; libraries are broadly divided into four types and they are:

I. Academic Library,

II. Special Library,

III. Public Library, and

IV. National Library.

I .Academic Library:

Academic library is the library which is attached to academic institutions like schools, colleges and universities. An academic library serves more specifically the students, research scholars, teachers and staff of the academic institution. Main objective of an academic library is to give maximum learning materials to its clientele so that they may be fully educated in their respective level. Academic libraries are again categorized into three types .They are:

1. School Library: A school library is a learning laboratory, providing a variety of instructional media, essential for optimum support of the education programme. The purpose of the school library is to attain the objectives of the educational programme. It concerns with the development of effective methods of thinking, inculcation of social attitudes, acquisition of important information and promoting growth and development among the children. The function of the school library is to help the students in the process of their self-discovery, to adopt high ideals in life, improve scholastic efficiency through self-study and to develop the capacity for critical thinking.

2. College Library:

College performs an important function in educational process. A college without a library is like a tree with no roots. The status of every college is measured through the position of the library that it maintains. Hence every college library should become a teaching instrument in itself. A college library is expected to support the objectives of the college. Thus, the basic function of a college library is to assist its parent body to carry out its programmers.

3. University Library:

A library is more important in a University, because a library can do without a University where as a university cannot function without a library. A university library is an integral part of the institution. It is primarily maintained for the benefit of students, officers, faculty members and for those who are engaged in research work. It plays a very important role in the national life of the community by acquiring material for educational use for the benefit of students and teaching departments.

II. Special Library:

Special library became popular since the beginning of 20th century. A special library is one which serves a particular group of people, such as the employees of a firm of government department, or the staff and members of a professional or research organization. Such a library deals essentially in information .

III.   Public Library:

A public library (also called circulating library) is a library which is accessible by the public and is generally funded from public sources (such as tax money) and may be operated by the civil servants. Taxing bodies for public libraries may be at any level from local to national central government level. The public library is an excellent model of government at its best. A locally controlled public good, it serves every individual freely, in as much or as little depth as he or she wants.

IV.   National Library:

A national library is a library specifically established by the government of a country to serve as the preeminent repository of information for that country. Unlike public libraries, these rarely allow citizens to borrow books. Often, they include numerous rare, valuable, or significant works. A National Library is that library which has the duty of collecting and preserving the literature of the nation within and outside the country, Thus, National Library are those libraries whose community is the nation at large.

Importance of Library

A Library is a communal place so adds to the importance of community in our lives. A library offers us education, relaxation and access to all sorts of books, magazines, music and movies that we could never afford to buy. It is a safe place to meet friends, use the internet or get help with school assignments. It is a place where all walks of life may be present including children, youth, and the aged. In an era where sustainability is becoming a necessity, a library is a provider.

A library has a great importance of its own. For a person of average means, it is difficult to purchase more than one or two daily newspapers or monthly magazines, but it is the keen desire of educated people to know all possible shades of opinion as expressed in different newspapers. Also, it is not possible to buy every book that you are interested to read. Hence library provides an effective alternate where you need to pay in a small number of membership fees and you can get to access to a variety of books, newspapers and magazines etc.

Library at home is a great way to keep your favorite reads organized in one place, without them lying around the apartment in messy heaps but it is not possible to have a library at home and also not affordable. Technology has taken over our lives and everything seems to be attainable digitally and so is the information sources. The sad part about online books is that the realness of holding one in your hands is lost. Also, these may cause a great amount of strain on our eyes, though it may be of convenience to constant travelers, there's nothing like a great book that you can leaf through, as opposed to clicking through. It's a relief how libraries are still going strong among those who love good old books. Love for reading doesn't die so easily, even if you are a follower of technology. Libraries play a very healthy role throughout our life. Libraries provide the students very healthy environment for learning as well as making notes or completing an assignment. Library provides a very calm and disciplined atmosphere which helps students to maintain a good concentration on their studies. Also, students can take reference books which can help them to make some quality notes. Libraries are the only place where we are free from all conventions because reading is absolutely a matter of personal choice. Readers are allowed to read what they like and also read the book according to their own manner. Nobody would check them or disturb them. Since everything is systematic and the atmosphere is calm so students can gain more in less time. One can save time and energy studying in libraries.

Conclusion

Libraries are one of the few places in the world that give all people a chance to improve themselves. There are a lot of activities that you can do there. People can learn about, how to find a job, fix their house. It isn't easy, and you still have to work hard. You have to know English, and you have to spend many hours at it. You can make use of different newspapers and employment news to find a job for you. Different books to study and a lot more is there in the library for everyone. Library offers a door for one and all, of every age group. Libraries offer free education and entertainment to the masses. It doesn't matter what your economic status is, you can come in and have free access to books that can inform and transform you.

Chapter 2

Library Administration and Management

By and large administering Libraries may appear simple task, especially when it comes to administering a larger institution like, university or college of higher education of which Library is just simply one small component or a sub-institution. Administration and management of each individual sub-institution of a larger establishment is as important as the establishment itself because an establishment can never function efficiently in absence of its well administered and efficiently managed sub-Institutions. Libraries since being one of the important and integral components of any larger educational establishment need to be administered and managed very well.

Definition of *Library Administration and Management*

According to Wikipedia, the on line free encyclopedia "**Library management** is a sub-discipline of institutional management that focuses on specific issues faced by libraries and library management professionals. Library management encompasses normal managerial tasks, as well as intellectual freedom and fundraising responsibilities. Issues faced in library management frequently overlap with those faced in managing non-profit organizations".[1]The basic functions of library management include, but are not limited to: planning and negotiating the acquisition of materials, Interlibrary Loan (ILL) requests, stacks maintenance, overseeing fee collection, event planning, fundraising, and human resources.[2]Library Administration handles internal and external administrative matters for the Libraries, providing managerial leadership, strategic planning, resource management, development/fundraising, and direction of the overall operations of the University Libraries

1 Acquisition

Acquisition of documents is one of the basic functions associated with any library. A library must acquire and provide all the relevant documents to its users within its budgetary limitations. An acquisition subsystem performs four basic operations. They are selection, ordering, receiving and accessioning of documents. Let us try and understand as to how these operations are performed in a library.

Selection

Selection of documents for library users is a very responsible job and should be based on definite principles and accepted norms. For a given library the book budget is limited and it should be spent judiciously to provide services to an optimum number of library users. Therefore, book selection becomes necessary. There are a number of tools (such as bibliographies, publisher's catalogues, etc.) which will be useful to library staff in the selection process. Requests from library users and suggestions from library authority are also considered for selection purposes. Such selections of documents need the approval of the competent authority, before they are ordered for purchase in the library.

Ordering

This procedure starts with pre-order searching, especially to avoid duplicate orders. In the next stage, purchase orders are generated and placed either directly to the respective publishers or to the list of vendors duly approved by the competent authority. Additionally, generation of reminders for overdue items and cancellation of orders also comes under the purview of ordering procedure.

Receiving

Documents and invoices or bills usually arrive together. Bills are checked with the order list before processing for payment. Newly arrived books are tallied with the bills and the order list to check whether the books received are as per the order and the author, title, edition, imprints and price are correct before accessioning. It is essential to ensure that books are not defective in any way before accessioning

Accessioning

A stock register is maintained by libraries in which all the documents purchased or received in exchange or as gift are recorded. Each document is provided with a consecutive serial number. The register is called Accession Register and the serial number to each document is referred to as Accession Number of the document. Accession register is one of the important records of the library. All the above mentioned procedures and related activities of the acquisition subsystem can be mechanized through 'library management software'. In such a system these basic activities are linked with the files of publishers, suppliers, budget and fund accounting, currency, etc. These files are maintained in computer-readable form and are utilized appropriately.

Processing

The processing procedure is the pivot around which all the housekeeping operations revolve in a library. Processing helps in the transformation of a library collection into serviceable resources. The procedures under this subdivision are classification, cataloguing, labeling and shelving.

Classification of Documents

Classification is grouping similar objects together. This principle is used to organize documents in libraries according to their subject content. It forms the foundation of librarianship. The following are the important classification schemes (aka systems) , which are used in different libraries of the world: Dewey Decimal Classification (DDC), Universal Decimal Classification (UDC), Library of Congress Classification (LC), Colon Classification (CC) and Subject Classification (SC), etc. The purposes for classifying of documents are: to help a user to find a document whose call number (i.e., class number + bookλ number) s/he knows. The class number represents the subject of a book while the book number individualises it among books on the same subject. to find out all the documents on a given subject.λ Classification is a mental process and demands intellectual exercises from a classifier. As a result, automatic synthesis of class numbers requires the application of Artificial Intelligence (AI) techniques in the development of software. In India, some research work on this topic has already been carried out at DRTC, Bangalore for building class numbers (based on Colon Classification) automatically through a software (called Vasya), written in PROLOG (PROgraming in LOGic) – a non-procedural programming language

Cataloguing

All these cataloguing procedures start with technical reading of the document to be catalogued by studying title, sub-title, alternate title, author, editor, edition, reprint, imprint, dedication, preface, table of contents, collation, series, bibliographies, etc. In case of manual cataloguing, the cataloguer makes separate cards for author; title, subject, cross-references and analytical entries by following any standard catalogue code (such as AACR-2, CCC, etc.) and file them as per the rules laid down by the library. Computerized cataloguing begins with entering bibliographical data of a book in a predesigned worksheet. The worksheet or datasheet is very similar to a data entry form and is based on any standard bibliographic record format (such as MARC 21, CCF, UNIMARC, etc.). Finally bibliographical data recorded in the worksheets are entered into the computer to produce a machine-readable catalogue file and OPAC. Computer based cataloguing supports importing of bibliographical records for the library resources either from centralized cataloguing service agency or from other libraries. Computer based cataloguing also supports exporting of bibliographical data of its own collection to other library systems. This facility reduces unit cost of cataloguing and ensures standardisation in cataloguing. The recent trend of cataloguing is to utilise Z39.50 protocol to download bibliographical data from other libraries and to provide global access to its own collection through Web OPAC.

Labeling

It is the work of pasting various labels on different parts of a document. The following labels are generally pasted in books:

Spine label:

This is done to make call number (a combination of class number and book number) properly visible to the users when the book is shelved. The size of the label is in the range of 1.25"×1.25".

Ownership slip/mark:

These are generally pasted on the inner side of the front cover at left hand top most corner. Ownership marks are put at various parts of a document by rubber stamps. The size of slip is 3"×2.5".

Date slip:

It is pasted on the top most portion of the front or back flyleaf of each book. The size of date slip is 5"×3"

Book pocket:

On the bottom of the inner right side of the front or back cardboard cover a book pocket is pasted.

Book card:

One printed/hand-written book card of size 5"×3" is put in the book pocket of each book

Shelving

Shelving is the arrangement of documents on the shelves to fulfill the fourth law of library science – Save time of the reader. Generally books are arranged on the shelves in a classified order as per the call number. Bound volumes of periodicals are generally shelved alphabetically by title and then by volume numbers.

Circulation

Most libraries lend books and other library materials to be read elsewhere by users. This is convenient for the users; this increases the use made of library collections and reduces the demand on reading space within library building. This function requires some sort of record keeping of what has been lent and to whom. The reasons for keeping loan records are:

.To minimize the loss of library materials; and

.To help library staff to answer users' queries about the location of items not on the shelves

A variety of systems for record keeping of loans have come into being based on needs. These are known as circulation systems. These involve some common jobs for successful implementation such as enrolment of members, issue and return of library documents, reservation of documents, renewal of documents, maintenance of documents and records, maintenance of statistics, inter-library loan, issuing of gate pass, etc. In a computer based circulation system, the machine-readable file consists of records for all items on loan from the library updated periodically with new records. This file is called "transaction file" and it takes required data from other two files – "document file" and "borrower file". Modern library management software support barcode based circulation system. In such a system, a barcode reader scans barcode for accession number of a document and the barcode in turn acts as a pointer to the document file. It helps to minimize labor and error in data entry operation. The concept of RFID (Radio Frequency Identification) based circulation system is emerging rapidly in developed countries. It comprises three components: a tag, a reader and an antenna. The tag contains important bibliographical data. The reader decodes the information stored on the chip after receiving it through the antenna and sends data to the central server to communicate library automation system. RFID technology supports patron self-checkout machines and has the ability to conduct inventory counts without removing a single book from the shelves. As a whole, RFID improves library workflow, staff productivity and customer service.

Serials Control

Serials in general and periodicals in particular are essential for research and development (R&D) activities. These are the primary means of communication for the exchange of scientific information. The periodicals or journals subscribed by libraries can be grouped into the following categories

.Indexing/Abstracting periodicals

.Periodicals containing news items

.Periodicals containing full-text research articles and technical papers

Acquisition of serials/periodicals in a library is different from book ordering system. In contrast to books, the libraries regularly subscribe periodicals against advance payment. The modes of subscription of periodicals in a library are as follows:

.Through local vendors/subscription agents

. Through foreign vendors/subscription agents

.Direct from the publishers

.As gift or complementary

.Through membership

.In exchange

.The fundamental tasks of any serials control system, manual or mechanized, can be listed as below:

1) Selection of serials

2) Selection of subscription mode

3) Formulation of terms of procurement

4) Selection of vendors

5) Order

6) Advance payment

7) Receiving and registration of serials issues in kardex

8) Sending reminders in case of issues not received

9) Adjustment of advance payment for missing issues

10) Preparation of list of subscribed journals, new arrivals and serials holdings for consultation by users

11) Binding and accessioning of back volumes of serials

In an automated system all these tasks are performed by library management software efficiently. It reduces workload of library staff. Computer based serials control systems may be predictive or non-predictive. Predictive systems predict the arrival of individual journal issues and can generate reminders in case of non-receipted issues. Prediction means the ability to inform that a named issue of a named journal will arrive in the library within a stated time interval. Modern library management software supports predictive mode of serials control with the facilities of online acquisition and access of journals through World Wide Web (WWW).

Maintenance If we don't take proper care to organize and administer the library documents regularly, these documents would become unserviceable resources immediately. The workflow of the maintenance division/section includes following tasks:

Shelf Rectification: It is to shelve misplaced documents in proper locations

Bind: It is to preserve library resources for future and present use

Replace: It is to replace a lost document by the library

Discard/Withdrawn: It is to weed out out-dated and torn and soiled documents from the library for making enough space for usable stock

Chapter 3
Library Classification

Library classification is an aspect of <u>library and information science</u>. It is distinct from <u>scientific classification</u> in that it has as its goal to provide a useful ordering of documents rather than a theoretical organization of <u>knowledge</u>. Although it has the practical purpose of creating a physical ordering of documents, it does generally attempt to adhere to accepted scientific knowledge. Library classification is distinct from the application of <u>subject headings</u> in that classification organizes knowledge into a systematic order, while subject headings provide access to intellectual materials through vocabulary terms that may or may not be organized as a knowledge system. The characteristics that a bibliographic classification demands for the sake of reaching these purposes are: a useful sequence of subjects at all levels, a concise memorable notation, and a host of techniques and devices of number synthesis·

Classification is one of the oldest and most prominent knowledge organizational tools. It used in Libraries, Information centers, and other institutions for organizing books, journals, newspaper, thesis, magazine etc. It is a system by which library materials are arranged according to subjects or class numbers or author of the books. Library Classification system uses a notational system that represents the order of the subject on the library and help users to easily finds materials on the shelves. It brings same subjects books together and separate unrelated subjects

The English term 'Classification' is a derivation from the Latin word "Classis" which connotes 'Grouping'. Classification is a procedure of grouping similar items and objects and is essential in formulating groups that is known as classifying which results in Classification. This process helps the user to arrange, organize and make a logical sense of articles which also assists the user to locate them in an easy manner. Classification is the ability to distinguish objects through their similarities and dissimilarities which is distinct in their identities for human beings.

Library classification – the systematic arrangement of books and other materials on shelves or of catalogue and index entries in the manner which is most useful to those who read or who seek a definite piece of information on a library.

Definitions of Library Classification:

The definitions of Library Classification are as follows:

According to Berwick Sayers, library classification is "the arrangement of books on shelves or descriptions of them, in the manner which is most useful to those who read."

Library Classification is meant to be "the translation of the name of the subject of a book into a preferred artificial language of ordinal numbers, and the individualization of the several books dealing with the same specific subject by means of further set of ordinal numbers which represent some features of the book other than their thought content." -Dr. S R Ranganathan

According to Margaret Mann, classification is "the arranging of things according to likeness and unlikeness. It is the sorting and grouping of things, but in addition classification of books is a knowledge classification with adjustment made necessary by the physical forms of books."

History

Library classifications were preceded by classifications used by bibliographers such as Conrad Gessner. The earliest library classification schemes organized books in broad subject categories. The earliest known library classification scheme is the Pinakes by Callimachus, a scholar at the Library of Alexandria during the Third Century BCE .After the printing revolution in the sixteenth century, the increase in available printed materials made such broad classification unworkable, and more granular classifications for library materials had to be developed in the nineteenth century. Although libraries created order within their collections from as early as the fifth century B.C.,[5] the Paris Bookseller's classification, developed in 1842 by Jacques Charles Brunet, is generally seen as the first of the modern book classifications. Brunet provided five major classes: theology, jurisprudence, sciences and arts, belles-lettres, and history.

Types

There are many standard systems of library classification in use, and many more have been proposed over the years. However, in general, classification systems can be divided into three types depending on how they are used:

Universal schemes which cover all subjects, for example the Dewey Decimal Classification, Universal Decimal Classification and Library of Congress Classification

Specific classification schemes which cover particular subjects or types of materials, for example Iconclass, British Catalogue of Music Classification, and Dickinson classification, or the NLM Classification for medicine.

National schemes which are specially created for certain countries, for example the Swedish library classification system, SAB (Sveriges Allmänna Biblioteksförening).

In terms of functionality, classification systems are often described as:

Enumerative: subject headings are listed alphabetically, with numbers assigned to each heading in alphabetical order.

Hierarchical: subjects are divided hierarchically, from most general to most specific.

Faceted or analytico-synthetic: subjects are divided into mutually exclusive orthogonal facets

There are few completely enumerative systems or faceted systems; most systems are a blend but favoring one type or the other. The most common classification systems, LCC and DDC, are essentially enumerative, though with some hierarchical and faceted elements (more so for DDC), especially at the broadest and most general level. The first true faceted system was the Colon classification of S. R. Ranganathan.

Library Classification can also be considered to be a process of putting books and other reading material on a subject in a logical sequence on the shelf, which could be of immense help to the users. It requires an adept thorough study and practice in the technique of classification of books, knowledge of the details and handling of the scheme of classification.

Components of Library Classification:

Library Classification is a process of translating the specific subject of a book into inartificial language of ordinal numbers, which in classificatory language are helpful in arriving at a logical arrangement. The essential components of a scheme of library classification are:

1. **Notation:** It is a set of symbols which stands for a class or a subject e.g. philosophy and literature and its sub-division example ethics, English literature representing a scheme of classification. For the purpose of arranging books, use of names of the subjects, broad or specific in natural language would neither be practicable nor convenient so these are translated into artificial language of ordinal numbers.

2. **Form Division:** Knowledge may be presented in one form of the other; the form could be text book, manual, history, dictionary and encyclopedia. These forms or styles of presenting knowledge of a subject could be commonly applied to any subject. Book classification takes care of representing form in the Call Number. The numbers representing the forms of books are called form divisions. They are also known as common sub-divisions or common-isolates.

3. **Generalia Class:** There are certain books such as encyclopedias, bibliographies and collected writings of an author which cannot be classified under any specific subject since they cover all subjects under the sun and hence are classified under the Generalia Class.

4. **Index:** Index is an essential component of a scheme of Library Classification which is provided at the end of the scheme. It is of immense value to the members in their handling of a classified part of the catalogue.

5. **Call Number:** In classifying, each book is provided with a distinguished number specified to it which can be used for calling the book from the stats and replacing it on its return to its right place. It is known as a Call Number.

Objectives of Library Classification

The objectives of library classification are given bellow:

1. **It brings like books together:** Classification arranges books in an order most convenient to the readers and the librarians. Readers should find all the related books together and librarians should minimum time and energy in locating the documents. Classification brings together all the books on the same subject. Not only that, books

on different branches of the subjects are also collated in a way that their mutual relationship is clearly displayed.

2. **It saves time:** Classification is a great time saving device for readers, as well as librarians and thus fulfils the demand of the fourth law of library science. The arrangement by subject, a natural consequence of library classification, saves a lot of time of readers as well as of staff, by bringing together all the related documents.

3. **It reveals the weakness and strength of the collection:** As classification arranges books on shelf by subject, it clearly shows which subjects have a good collection, and which subjects require more attention. In this way, it facilitates the book selection process and helps in developing all round collection of the library. Similarly, it assists the librarians in making up their collection, for the departmental or branch libraries or lending centers, from the central stock.

4. **It helps in bibliographic research:** Classification is of value in bibliographic research as it helps in the compilation of bibliographies, catalogues and union catalogues.

5. **It helps in stock verification:** Classification plays a significant role in the stock taking procedure. Generally, verification of stock is done through a shelf list, which is arranged in classified order. Books on the shelf are also arranged in the same order. In the stock taking procedure, a person on the shelf goes on calling the call number of the books while the other person, holding the shelf list goes on pushing the relevant cards forward. Thus, the process of stock taking is completed within a relatively short time

Purpose of Library Classification

The following are the main purposes of library classification:

1. Helpful Sequence:

Classification helps in organizing the documents in a method most convenient to the users and to the library staff. The documents should be systematically arranged in classes based on the mutual relationship between them which would bring together all closely related classes. The basic idea is to bring the like classes together and separate these from unlike classes. The arrangement should be such that the user should be able to retrieve the required document as result it will make a helpful sequence.

2. Correct Replacement:

Documents whenever taken out from shelf should be replaced in their proper places. It is essential that library classification should enable the correct replacement of documents after they have been returned from use. This would require a mechanized arrangement so that arrangement remains permanent.

3. Mechanized Arrangement:

It means to adopt a particular arrangement suitable for the library so that the arrangement remains permanent. The sequence should be determined once for all, so that one does not have to pre-determine the sequence of documents once again when these are returned after being borrowed.

4. Addition of New Document:

Library would acquire new documents from time to time therefore library classification should help in finding the most helpful place for each of those among the existing collection of the library. There are two possibilities in this regard. The new books may be or a subject already provided for in the scheme of library classification, or it may be or a newly emerging subject that may not have been provided in the existing scheme.

5. Withdrawal of Document from Stock:

In this case, the need arises to withdraw a document from the library collection for some reason, and then library classification should facilitate such a withdrawal.

6. Book Display:

Display is adopted for a special exhibition of books and other materials on a given topic. The term is used to indicate that the collection in an open access library is well presented and guided. Library classification should be helpful in the organization of book displays.

7. Other Purposes:

- For compilation of bibliographies catalogues and union catalogues.
- For Classification of information.
- For Classification of reference queries.
- For Classification of suggestions received from the users.
- For Filing of non book materials such as photographs, films, etc

Features of Library Classification Scheme

The library Classification schemes need to include the following features to prove to be of maximum benefit to the classifier:

1. Schedules:

The term Schedule is used to describe the printed list of all the main classes, divisions and sub-divisions of the classification scheme. They provide a logical arrangement of all the subjects encompassed by the classification scheme. This arrangement usually being hierarchical shows the relationship of specific subjects to their parent subject. The relevant classification symbol is shown against each subject.

2. Index:

The Index to the classification scheme is an alphabetical list of all the subjects encompassed by the scheme, with the relevant class mark shown against each subject. There are two types of index:

- **A Relative Index:** includes broad topics in its alphabetic arrangement, but indented below the broad subject heading is a list of all the aspects of the subject. For e.g. Dewey Decimal Classification Scheme has an excellent relative index.
- **A Specific Index:** lists specific subjects in a précis alphabetical sequence. It does not indent lists of related topics under the broad subject headings. For example, Brown's Subject Classification Scheme has a specific index.

3. Notation:

Notation is the system of symbols used to represent the terms encompassed by the classification scheme. The notation can be pure – using one type of symbol only – or mixed – using more than one kind of symbol. A pure notation would normally involve only letters of the alphabet or only numerals. A mixed notation would normally utilize both letters and numerals. Some notations also involve the use of grammatical signs or mathematical symbols. The notation usually appears on the spines of library books to facilitate shelving and to ensure that each book is in its correct place. The notation is also shown on catalogue entries to help the staff and public to remove books quickly. It therefore serves as:

- A link between the index and the schedules of a classification scheme, and
- A link between the library catalogues and the shelves.

4. Tables:

The tables of a classification scheme are additional to the schedules and provide lists of symbols which can be added to class marks to them more specific and precise.

5. Form Class:

A form class makes provision for those books where form is of greater importance than subject. Most books of this kind are literary works– fiction, poetry, plays etc.

6. A Generalities Class:

This class caters primarily for books of General knowledge which could not be allocated to any particular subject class due to their pervasive subject coverage. In some respects, a generalities class is also a form class since general bibliographies

CONCLUSION

"Library is grooving organism. " Hence for update of knowledge every library needs the new books/documents. Library classification arrange the all documents in libraries and information centers on the racks very systematically .Nowadays classification is widely adopted and is considered as very important to several organization of information management. Library is one of common organization who adopts classification. ... Such an arrangement is used for reader's benefit when they wanted to search for particular book.

Chapter 4

LIBRARY CATALOGUE:

Introduction

Library catalogue is an essential and important tool for any library. This tool has been developed to facilitate the use of reading materials in a library. It is useful to both, the readers using the library and the library staff members who help the readers to use the library. Library catalogue is a list of books and other reading materials available in a particular library. It discloses to the reader the contents of a library collection. Whereas, cataloguing is a technique of describing the documents in order to help the reader to identify the document in which he is interested. In this Unit,, we introduce you to some of the basic ideas relating to library catalogues and cataloguing.. The objective in the preparation and production of a library catalogue is to assist; the users in identifying the contents of a library. The library catalogue guides the users to identify, locate and access reading and reference materials in the library. Essentially a library catalogue functions as a finding tool to know what a library has. A library catalogue lets a reader know if the library has a document for which the author or the subject or the exact title is known. In addition, it gives information regarding all the other books on a given author or all other books in a subject or a publisher's series or the different editions or translations of a given title available in the library. In the preparation of such a tool, a standard code or rules and procedures for cataloguing different kinds of documents guide cataloguers. Libraries also create a number of other records of documents acquired by them. Some of these are: accession register, the shelf register, current periodicals register, register for periodical holdings, etc. Much of the bibliographical data that go into these registers may be more or less the same as in a library catalogue. For instance, the accession register is an inventory of documents acquired by a library containing detailed information about the price, the vendor who supplied the document, size, in addition to the usual bibliographical data. The shelf register is a list of documents reflecting exactly the way documents are arranged on the shelves in different rooms or halls. It is useful for stock verification. They have some resemblance to a library catalogue but their functions are quite distinct and different. Library catalogues are also different from the publishers' catalogues, booksellers' lists, bibliographies, etc. Each of these reference tools is useful to build up the collections for a library book selection, but they do not do what a library catalogue does.

A modern library provides a number of facilities to its readers for making use of its collection. One such facility is the catalogue of the library which facilitates the readers to know what documents the library has, where they are located on library shelves, and how to access them. In this section, we shall discuss the definition, objectives and functions of a library catalogue.

Meaning &Definitions:

The word `catalogue' has been derived from the Greek expression `kata logos'. It means a list, register or complete enumeration of something. It has now come to mean a list of somethings, systematically arranged in alphabetical or other order, often with brief description of items listed. For example: A catalogue of items of furniture for sale in an auction; a catalogue of different kinds of pumps manufactured by a particular company. The New English Dictionary defines a catalogue as follows: 'A catalogue is usually distinguished from a mere list or enumeration by systematic or methodic arrangement, alphabetical or other order and often by the addition of brief particulars, descriptive or aiding identification, indicative of locality, position, date, price or the like'. In the context of a library, a catalogue is a list of books and other documents of a particular library. This list is arranged according to a definite order, containing specific bibliographic data for the purpose of identification and location of the documents catalogued. A formal definition of a library catalogue is that it is an explanatory, logically arranged inventory and key to the documents and their contents and it is confined to the documents of a particular library. It the catalogue represents the collection of two or more libraries, the catalogue is termed as union catalogue. Harrod's librarians' glossary and reference book 6th edition, has defined catalogue as `a list of books, maps, or other items, arranged in definite order. It records, describes and indexes (usually completely) the resources of a collection, a library or a group of libraries. Each entry bears details of class number or call number to enable the item to he found (on the shelves of the library), as well as sufficient details (such as author, title, editorship, place of publication, publisher, date of publication, edition pages, illustrations) to identify and describe a book. To be distinguished from (1) a list, which may or may not be in any particular order and may be incomplete, and (2) a bibliography, which may not be confined to any one collection of books or to a particular group of libraries'.

'To catalogue' means to compile a list of documents according to a set of rules (i.e., according to a catalogue code) so as to enable the reader to know what items (documents) are available in the library, and where this document can be found on the shelves of the library with the help of the class number, call number or other means of identification given in the catalogue entry. Dr. S. R. Ranganathan has defined the term library catalogue as a list of the documents in a library or in a collection forming a-portion of it. He further states, `A catalogue may be printed, or it may be in manuscript form. It may be in cards or in loose leaves. It may be in the form of a continuous book or in the paste down form with gaps for the interpolation of new entries in between existing entries'. (Ch. FM, CCC, Ed 5).

Purposes of a Library Catalogue:

Libraries generally acquire reading and reference materials in various physical forms, which will be utilised by users for study, reference, research and other purposes. These materials are constantly under consultation or in circulation and therefore, at any given point of time, some of these materials may not be available on the shelves in the library. These reading and reference materials may also be in different physical forms such as printed documents, microfilms or machine-readable forms. They are located and shelved at different place such as sections, rooms, floors in the library, depending upon the most appropriate form of storage. Because of these reasons, it is necessary that a library prepares and provides a public record of all the materials irrespective of their physical forms-acquired. by it in order to give the readers an idea of the entire collection possessed by it. So the main objective of a library catalogue is to aid readers in making use of the collection of the library by providing author, subject, title and other approaches to the collection. The primary purpose of a library catalogue is to serve as a guide to the collection of materials. Basically, it reveals to the users the document or non- document materials contained in the library and aids them in finding out whether the materials of their interest are available in the library or not. In other words, a library catalogue serves as a key to the library collection as well as location or as a retrieval tool.

Objectives of a Library Catalogue

Charles Ami Cutter described the objectives of a library catalogue in 1876 when he published the first edition of his book Rules for a

Dictionary Catalogue. His views on the subject are often quoted and are relevant even today. According to him, a catalogue should:

1) Enable a person to find out a document of which

a) The author, or

b) The title, or

c) The subject is known

2) Show to users what the library has

d) By a given author

e) On a given subject

f) In a given kinds of literature

3) Assist users in the choice of a document

g) As to its edition (bibliographically).

h) As to its character (literary or topical)

All the above mentioned objectives are valid even today. As a library today acquires various types of reading and reference materials, it may be necessary to replace the word `book' by. `Document' representing paper-print material as well as microforms and machine-readable forms. The first objective of a library catalogue is to inform the availability/non availability of a particular reading material in the library. The readers may approach the catalogue through the name of an author or title. The author or title entry should provide the reader all the pertinent information. In case the entry is under some other name or word, a cross-reference entry should be provided. The title entries in the catalogue cater to the title approach of the readers. The name of a subject is another access point. In a great number of cases, the reader does not approach or search the catalogue through the name of an author or title of a document. His interest is in a particular subject. In such cases the subject entry in the catalogue furnishes him the requisite information. The concepts of a subject may be described in varied terms. Only standardized terminology is used in preparing subject entries in a library catalogue. The second objective is to show what a library has. The catalogue lists all the works of a particular author available in the library collection, all the documents available in a given subject or in a given kind of literature. The third objective is known as descriptive cataloguing. According to the rules of descriptive cataloguing, the characteristics of the documents are fully described so that one document can be identified and isolated from amongst several similar documents. This type of description is .provided in the catalogue entries only in case of need. If the rules of descriptive cataloguing are applied indiscriminately, it would lead to large expenditure. In brief, whatever may be the approach of a library user, the library catalogue should convey full information regarding the items of the person's specific interest.

Functions of Library Catalogue:

The major functions of a library catalogue are:

1. Whether an information institution contains a certain book or other reading materials.

2. Which works by a particular author are in the collection.

3. Which materials the library has on a particular subject.

4. Which editions of a particular work the library has.

Apart from these four basic functions, a library catalogue is expected to broadly
perform the following functions:

1. To work as a book selection tool for other comparatively new or smaller library.

2. To explain a book to the reader by providing a description of each book.

3. To employ Cross references, i.e. See, and See also references.

4. To arrange the call numbers numerically and alphabetically by which books may be located or obtained.

5. To record each work in an information institution by author, editor, compiler, translator, series, or by corporate body.

6. To arrange author entries in such a way that a reader finds all the works of an author together in a dictionary catalogue.

7. To record each work in an information institution under the subject.

8. To arrange subject entries either according to classification number, or alphabetically by subject.

9. To record titles of work if it is (a) written by more than three authors, (b) a compiled or edited work including encyclopedias and dictionaries, (c) a fiction, or a popular work.

10. To help the research workers and readers know what materials are available on a given subject in the information institution

11) Library catalogue helps to ,Choice and rendering of headings of main entries,   added
          entries .

12) Library catalogue helps to recording of information in the sections of entries.

13) It also helps to determination of style of writing, punctuation marks, capitalization, etc.

14) For preparation of entries.

15)For writing call numbers on all the entries.

16)For filing of catalogue cards.

17) For preparation of guide cards.

18) For maintenance and updating of entries in a catalogue.

19) A library catalogue can also be used as a reference tool for answering many questions   of users of documents

Conclusion:

A library catalogue may be helpful in identifying know items or known works when some attributes can be used as search keys (e.g. author name or title). A catalogue may also be helpful in identifying not know items dealing with a particular subject such as World War II.
Hence, we can say that Library catalogue is the "Key " of searching the collection of particular library.

Chapter 5

Reference source/Book

What is a reference book?

A reference book is a source that provides facts &/or finite pieces of information; this can be general (*Encyclopedia Britannica*) or more subject focused (*Encyclopedia of Women and Baseball*). They are sources designed not to be read cover to cover but to be used to get key facts about a topic (think dictionary or almanac). These materials don't circulate (they have to be used in the Library) so that everyone can use the material. Reference books are a great place to start your research, find general history/background information as well as important people, dates &/or terms related to your topic.

Reference books are usually organized alphabetically (think encyclopedia or dictionary) but using the Index (the back section of a book or group of books that alphabetically lists the headings including people, places and subjects with corresponding page numbers) can be a quick way to find the information you need.

In our library reference books are located in the first eleven moving shelves and are marked with "reference collection" marked on a red sign on the end of the shelves. They are marked USC Upstate Reference in the catalog and have REF on the top of the spine label.

Reference books give you:

- A quick introduction to your subject by covering a lot of points briefly

- In-depth background on some of the major people &/or key elements of your topic
- Vocabulary to use for searches in other resources
- Ideas for additional resources (check the reference list)

Types of Reference Sources / Books

Reference sources such as dictionaries, encyclopedias, almanacs, atlases, etc. are research tools that can help you with your paper or project. Reference sources provide answers to specific questions, such as brief facts, statistics, and technical instructions; provide background information; or direct you to additional information sources. Reference sources are not scholarly (peer-reviewed). In most libraries, reference sources do not circulate and are located in a separate reference collection. This practice makes reference sources readily available and easily accessible.

Reference sources are designed to be consulted rather than read through. Reference materials can be arranged alphabetically, topically, or chronologically. Many will contain cross listed information and more than one index. If it is not obvious how a reference source is organized, take a moment to look through the explanatory or how-to-use information, which is usually presented at the beginning of the book, or in HELP screens for online products.

There are thousands of reference sources available that cover practically every subject. Although the term reference "book" is frequently used, reference sources can be books, serials, on-line databases or information found on the Internet. A large part of using reference sources well is choosing the right one for your needs.

Despite the wide variety available, reference sources can be categorized into a handful of groups. Think about the kind of information you need and how you will use it. If you are unsure which reference tool is best suited to your information need, a reference librarian will be able to assist the user

Types of Reference Tools

Two major categories of reference materials are general and subject. **General reference sources** include all subjects and present overviews of topics. **Subject's specific reference sources** provide in-depth coverage on specialized topics.

Dictionary

According to **Wikipedia, the free on line Encyclopedia** A **dictionary**, sometimes known as a **wordbook**, is a collection of words in one or more specific languages, often arranged alphabetically (or by radical and stroke for ideographic languages), which may include information on definitions, usage, etymologies, pronunciations, translation, etc.or a book of words in one language with their equivalents in another, sometimes known as a lexicon. It is a lexicographical product which shows inter-relationships among the data.

A broad distinction is made between general and specialized dictionaries. Specialized dictionaries include words in specialist fields, rather than a complete range of words in the language. Lexical items that describe concepts in specific fields are usually called terms instead of words, although there is no consensus whether lexicology and terminology are two different fields of study. In theory, general dictionaries are supposed to be semasiological, mapping word to definition, while specialized dictionaries are supposed to be onomasiological, first identifying concepts and then establishing the terms used to designate them. In practice, the two approaches are used for both types.[3]

Types of **Dictionary**

The types of dictionaries are given below :

- **General Dictionaries**

General dictionaries are the most familiar to us. You may even own one. This group includes *Webster's International Dictionary*, the *Random House Dictionary of the English Language*, and the Merriam-Webster Collegiate Dictionary. These sources generally provide definitions, pronunciations, syllabication, and usage.

- **Historical Dictionaries**

Historical dictionaries provide the history of a word from its introduction into the language to the present. *The Oxford English Dictionary* is an excellent example of this type of dictionary.

- **Etymological Dictionaries**

Etymological dictionaries are dictionaries which emphasize the anaylsis of components of words and their cognates in other languages. These dictionaries emphasize the linguistic and grammatical history of the word usage. The *Oxford Dictionary of English Etymology* is an example of an etymological dictionary.

Period or scholarly specialized Dictionaries

Period or scholarly specialized dictionaries focus on a particular place or time period. For example, try the *Dictionary of Alaskan English* if you would like to know when the word "cheechako" was first used.

Foreign language Dictionaries

Foreign language dictionaries are fairly self-explanatory. We've all looked up words in a French or Spanish or other Western European language. Don't forget other wonderful dictionaries, such as the *Yup'ik Eskimo Dictionary* or the *Inupiat Eskimo dictionary*.

Subject Dictionaries

Subject dictionaries focus on word definitions in a subject area, such as finance, law, botany, electronics, physics, etc.

Other Dictionaries

Other dictionaries include dictionaries of slang, abbreviations, synonyms, antonyms, abbreviations, acronyms, reversals, rhyming, idioms, phrases, and guides to correct usage. *Dictionary of Acronyms and Abbreviations, The Macmillan Dictionary of Historical Slang*, Roget's II: The New Thesaurus, The American Language, Strunk's Elements of Style.

Dictionaries, like other reference sources, may belong to more than one category. For example, an English-Russian engineering dictionary is both a foreign language and a subject dictionary.

Dictionaries may be abridged or unabridged. Abridged dictionaries are smaller and contained the most commonly used words. Unabridged dictionaries try to include all words in current usage. Like other reference sources, dictionaries may become outdated as language evolves. Care should be taken to carefully identify the publication date and focus of the dictionary selected. General dictionaries begin with LC call numbers starting with AG. Specialized dictionaries will have subject specific call numbers.

Encyclopedias

An **encyclopedia** or **encyclopaedia** is a reference work or compendium providing summaries of knowledge from either all branches or from a particular field or discipline. Encyclopedias are divided into articles or entries that are often arranged alphabetically by article name and sometimes by thematic categories. Encyclopedia entries are longer and more detailed than those in most dictionaries. Generally speaking, unlike dictionary entries which focus on linguistic information about words, such as their meaning, pronunciation, use, and grammatical forms, encyclopedia articles focus on factual information concerning the subject named in the article's title.

Encyclopedias provide general background information; they are a good place to start researching a topic that you know little about. Large subject areas or disciplines are covered in broad articles that explain basic concepts. These overview articles often contain references to more specific aspects of the larger topic and may include a bibliography that leads you to more in-depth sources. Encyclopedias may be general or subject specific.

Types of Encyclopedias

Types of Encyclopedias are given below:

General encyclopedias

General encyclopedias, usually arrange articles alphabetically by topic. Look for an accompanying index which may list cross-references to other articles. Included in this category are *Encyclopaedia Britannica, The Cambridge Encyclopedia, Encyclopedia Americana*, and the Columbia Encyclopedia. General encyclopedia LC call numbers begin with AE.

Subject encyclopedias

Subject encyclopedias are available for almost every academic discipline. They provide more in-depth and technical information than general encyclopedias. Subject encyclopedias generally assume some prior knowledge of the subject. There is no general rule for how these tools are arranged. Look for an index. A few examples of subject encyclopedias include the *McGraw-Hill Encyclopedia of Science and Technology, International Encyclopedia of the Social Sciences, Encyclopedia of World Art, Encyclopedia of Philosophy*, and the *Encyclopedia of Archaeology*. Subject encyclopedias will have subject specific call numbers.

Directories

In general directory means , a book or website listing individuals or organizations alphabetically or thematically with details such as names, addresses, and telephone numbers.

Directories provide names, addresses, affiliations, etc. of people, organizations, or institutions. They can be used to verify addresses, name spellings, and provide contact information. As in other reference sources, directories may be general or focused on a particular subject.

Types of **directories**

The types of directories are:

- *General directories*: Zip Code & Post Office Directory, Encyclopedia of Associations

- **Subject directories**: *Fairbanks Phone Directory, Museums of the World, A Directory of Eskimo Artists in Sculpture and Prints*, A-Z Index of U.S. Government Departments and Agencies, *Directory of Multinationals*, Thomas Register of American Manufacturers.

Biographical Dictionaries

A **biographical dictionary** is a type of encyclopedic dictionary limited to biographical information. Many attempt to cover the major personalities of a country (with limitations, such as living person's only, in Who's Who, or deceased people only, in the Dictionary of National Biography). Others are specialized, in that they cover important names in a subject field, such as architecture or engineering.

Biographical dictionaries contain short articles about people's lives. Biography resources have call numbers that begin with CT.

Types of Biographical Dictionaries

The Types of Biographical Dictionaries are:

1.General biographical dictionaries include *Current Biography, Dictionary of American Biography, Who's Who, Encyclopedia of World Biography*, etc.

2.Subject biographical dictionaries may focus on a subject area or group. These sources include *Dictionary of Scientific*

Biography, Contemporary Authors, Biographical Dictionary of Psychology , New Grove Dictionary of Music and Musicians, Women of Science, etc.

Gazetteers or Atlases

A **gazetteer** is a geographical dictionary or directory used in conjunction with a map or atlas.[1] It typically contains information concerning the geographical makeup, social statistics and physical features of a country, region, or continent. Content of a gazetteer can include a subject's location, dimensions of peaks and waterways, population, gross domestic product and literacy rate. This information is generally divided into topics with entries listed in alphabetical order.

Ancient Greek gazetteers are known to have existed since the Hellenistic era. The first known Chinese gazetteer was released by the first century, and with the age of print media in China by the ninth century, the Chinese gentry became invested in producing gazetteers for their local areas as a source of information as well as local pride. The geographer Stephanus of Byzantium wrote a geographical dictionary (which currently has missing parts) in the sixth century which influenced later European compilers. Modern gazetteers can be found in reference sections of most libraries as well as on the internet.

Geographic information is located in gazetteers, atlases and maps. Geography resources have call numbers that begin with G.

Types of Atlases

1.Atlases contain collections of maps. They provide information on geographical/political changes. There are world, national, and thematic atlases and these may be current or historical.

2.World atlases include *National Geographic Atlas of the World.*

3.National atlases: *National Atlas of the United States, Atlas of the American Revolution.*

4.Thematic atlases focus on a specific subject area, such as astronomy or agriculture. Examples include, *The Oxford Economic Atlas of the World* and the *Environmental Atlas of Alaska.*

Types of Gazetteers

Gazetteers are sometimes referred to as geographical dictionaries and provide descriptions of places, but no maps.

1.General gazetteers include *Webster's New Geographical Dictionary, The Columbia Lippincott Gazetteer of the World, Gazetteer of Undersea Features,* etc.

2.Regional gazetteers, such as *Dictionary of Alaska Place Names*, by D. Orth, focus on a specific geographical region and are good places to look if you want to know the location of a town, its population, or where its name came from.

Sometimes atlases and gazetteers are combined, as in the *Alaska Atlas and Gazetteer*, by DeLorme Mapping, which publishes similar products for the other states.

Almanacs

An **almanac** (also spelled *almanack* and *almanach*) is an annual publication listing a set of events forthcoming in the next year.It includes information like weather forecasts, farmers' planting dates, tide tables, and other tabular data often   arranged   according   to the calendar. Celestial figures and various statistics are found in almanacs, such   as   the rising and setting times   of   the Sun and Moon,   dates of eclipses, hours of high and low tides, and religious festivals.

A calendar, which is a system for time keeping, in written form is usually produced as a most simple almanac: it includes additional information about the day of the week on which a particular day falls, major holidays, the phases of the moon, earthquake hazard levels etc. The set of events noted in an almanac are selected in view of a more or less specific group of readers e.g. farmers, sailors, astronomers or others.

Almanacs contain statistics and facts about countries, events, personalities, or subjects. Almanac resources have call numbers that begin with AY.

Types of Almanacs

The types of Almanacs are:

1.General almanacs include the *Statistical Abstract of the United States*, *The New York Public Library Desk Reference*, *World Almanac* (an American focus), Information Please Almanac (print ed. called *Time Almanac*), *Whitaker's Almanak* (United Kingdom focus).

2.Subject almanacs include *The Weather Almanac*, *The Almanac of Renewable Energy*, *Political Reference Almanac*, *Alaska Almanac*, and more.

Year Book

A yearbook, also known as an **annual**, is a type of a book published annually to record, highlight, and commemorate the past year of a school. The term also refers to a book of statistics or facts published annually. A yearbook often has an overarching theme that is present throughout the entire book. Many high schools, colleges, and elementary and middle schools publish yearbooks; however, many schools are dropping yearbooks or decreasing page counts given social media alternatives to a mass-produced physical photographically-oriented record.From 1995 to 2013, the number of U.S. college yearbooks dropped from roughly 2,400 to 1,000.

Handbooks/Manuals

A Handbook is a type of <u>reference work</u>, or other collection of instructions, that is intended to provide ready reference. The term originally applied to a small or portable book containing information useful for its owner, but the <u>Oxford English Dictionary</u>defines the current sense as "any book...giving information such as facts on a particular subject, guidance in some art or occupation, instructions for operating a machine, or information for tourists.

Handbooks may deal with any topic, and are generally compendiums of information in a particular field or about a particular technique. They are designed to be easily consulted and provide quick answers in a certain area. For example, the <u>MLA Handbook for Writers of Research Papers</u> is a reference for how to cite works in MLA style, among other things. Examples of <u>engineering</u> handbooks include <u>Perry's Chemical Engineers' Handbook</u>, <u>Marks Standard Handbook for Mechanical Engineers</u>, and the <u>CRC Handbook of Chemistry and Physics</u>.

Handbooks and manuals are subject area tools. Handbooks provide facts, terms, concepts, movements, etc. of a topic. Manuals provide detailed instructions on a particular subject, such as how-to-do something or how something works.

For Ex: *Handbook of North American Indians, Guide to Alaska Trees, Words and Ideas: A Handbook for College Writing, Handbook of Mathematical Formulas, MLA Handbook For Writers of Research Papers.*

Manuals:

A **user guide** or **user's guide**, also commonly known as a **manual**, is a <u>technical communication</u> <u>document</u> intended to give assistance to people using a particular system.[1] It is usually written by a <u>technical writer</u>, although user guides are written by programmers, product or project managers, or other technical staff, particularly in smaller companies.

User guides are most commonly associated with electronic goods, computer hardware and software. Most user guides contain both a written guide and the associated images. In the case of computer applications, it is usual to include screenshots of the human-machine interface(s), and hardware manuals often include clear, simplified diagrams. The language used is matched to the intended audience, with jargon kept to a minimum or explained thoroughly.

For Ex: *Manual of Photography, Manual for Environmental Impact Evaluation, Alaska Craftsman Home Building Manual, United States Government Manual.*

Indexing sources

General indexing sources are a good place to start if your topic is popular, current, or if you only need basic information. One drawback of general indexes is that due to the nature of the magazines they include, you may find some less reliable and less informational articles, see "Evaluating Citations."

Listed below are a few of the general indexes which are available to you:

Readers' Guide to Periodical Literature (via EBSCOhost)
This was the standard periodical index for many years. It is available in print form and has been indexing journals since 1900. It can usually be found in the reference or index section of the library. An electronic version is also available, but coverage starts in 1983. It can be accessed through the Databases by Title page and clicking on Readers' Guide Abstracts.

EBSCOhost (via Digital Pipeline)
A "one-stop online reference system accessible via the Internet." EBSCOhost includes many individual databases which focus on topics like business, kids' interests, newspapers, academic research, health, and current events. Coverage ranges from general to academic levels, and the full-text of journal articles is included. Access EbscoHost from the SLED homepage by clicking "Magazines, Newspapers, and More: Full

Text Articles for Alaskans" or through the Rasmuson Library and clicking "Alaska resources via SLED".

Article1st (via OCLC FirstSearch)
Article1st is an OCLC index of articles from the contents pages of journals. It can be accessed through the Databases by Title.

ECO (Electronic Collections Online) - (via OCLC FirstSearch)
Access abstracts and full-text articles in more than 5,400 publications covering a wide range of subjects. It can be accessed through the Databases by Title.

Abstracting sources

An abstract is a brief summary of a research article, thesis, review, conference proceeding, or any in-depth analysis of a particular subject and is often used to help the reader quickly ascertain the paper's purpose. When used, an abstract always appears at the beginning of a manuscript or typescript, acting as the point-of-entry for any given academic paper or patent application. Abstracting and indexing services for various academic disciplines are aimed at compiling a body of literature for that particular subject.

Types of Abstract

Informative abstract,

The **informative abstract,** also known as the **complete abstract,** is a compendious summary of a paper's substance including its background, purpose, methodology, results, and conclusion. Usually between 100 and 200 words, the informative abstract summarizes the paper's structure, its major topics and key points A format for scientific short reports that is similar to an informative abstract has been proposed in recent years.[11] Informative abstracts may be viewed as standalone documents.

Descriptive abstract

The **descriptive abstract,** also known as the **limited abstract** or the **indicative abstract,** provides a description of what the paper covers without delving into its substance.[12] A descriptive abstract is akin to a <u>table of contents</u> in paragraph form.

Bibliographies

Bibliographies lead to other information sources. They are lists of books and other materials that provide author, title, and publication information. Annotated bibliographies also include a brief description or summary of the item. Bibliographies are available on almost every topic and may focus on specific persons, groups, subjects, or time periods. Many bibliographies are selective and do not attempt to include all publications. Bibliographies are sometimes referred to as "Guides to the Literature ..."

Examples: *American Fiction, 1774-1850, Bibliography of Education, Utilization of Wood Residues: An Annotated Bibliography, A Bibliography of Sir Walter Scott, MLA Bibliography, Current Bibliographies in Medicine* (NLM), <u>Alutiiq Ethnographic Bibliography</u> (ANKN) Indian National Bibliography(INB)

Chapter **6**

Library and Information services

INTRODUCTION

The literature on library and information science/services indicates that Libraries started off as store houses, where books were more preserved than utilized and librarians acted like some form of custodians and their interaction with users were minimal, for example only in locating books and serving users, then there was a shift as a result of information communication technology. Librarians were supposed to be custodians who did not encourage the use of books. The users were expected to use the library on their own. At most, if a user asked for a book, then the service that would be offered by the so called librarian was to pass on the book and leave the user alone. From the ancient times to present we note that this trend in services has tremendously changed to due information technology.

Libraries play different roles for different people. To some, a library is a place to read books; be furnished with the current news from up-to-date newspapers; to do research; a place to access or share information in response to a particular need; etc. Now days, libraries and librarians play an important role in providing access to information, organizing it, and helping users to find the information they need. Consequently, information services have become a key element for libraries. The present user's interest is to get the information in need within a given timeframe. The timeframe varies with the user's mission or task. For example the timeframe for a surgeon preparing for an operation before entering a theater is much shorter and critical than that of a teacher preparing for the next lecture. Though the present users can get access to the vast amount of information on the Internet and online databases, the role of library information services has no where reduced. The amount and diversity of the ever-increasing information on the Internet and in online databases is one of the major attributes to the increased role of library information service units. The lack of information organization on the web; the demands of users who want quicker and clear answers in response to their information needs; technological skill deficiency among some information seekers to efficiently and effectively search for the right information; are among the few causes that have raised the need for information services more than before in libraries.

.

Definition

An **InformationService** is a service, which provides (*serves*) *data/knowledge/information* somehowHowever, this definition is not strong enough to describe the range and domain of an *Information Service*. Therefore, it is necessary to define the term *Information Service* in a specific context. Fortunately, *Wikipedia* delivers, or better saying **serves**, a good definition of this context, which is called *Information System*.

An **Information System** is any *combination* of *information technology* and *people*'s activities using that technology to support operations, management, and decision-making.

The definition continues with explaining the term from a bit more *technical* view:
In a very broad sense, the term *Information System* is frequently used to refer to the *interaction* between people, algorithmic processes, *data* and technology

Regarding the first part of this definition, an *Information Service* is an instance of *Information Technology*. Hence, an *Information Service* is a part of an *Information System*. The second role in this definition is *people*. This term must be substituted by the term *agent*, which could be an *administrator* and/or an *user*. An *user* could be a *customer* and/or *contributor*. In addition, an *agent* could be a *human* or a *machine*. The *interaction*s that an *Information Service*, which *collects* (retrieves), *manages* (structures) & *stores* the *data/knowledge/information* (maybe with the help of

an *administrator*), *serves* this *data/knowledge/information* to   an *user*.
The outcome of this is the definition: An **Information Service** is this part of an *Information*
System that *servesdata/knowledge/information** to *customers* and *collects* i
t   from   its *contributors*,   to *manage* and *store* it   by   optionally
using *administrators*.

Information / Documentation services

The documentation/Information service is based or dependent on documents. The word is used in the broader sense by those working with collection of data or information of any kind. In the restricted sense, as used by historians, documentation/information service is citation of written evidence in support of a statement, while according to liberal sense, documentation covers all action related to documents from identification to dissemination. The important library & information services are given below :

CURRENT AWARENESS SERVICES (CAS)

CAS has been defined by D.A kemp as: system for reviewing newly available documents, selecting items relevant to the needs of an individual or group, and recording them so that notifications may be sent to those individuals or groups to whose need they are related. In a nutshell, CAS is a technique for communicating information in such a manner as to keep each researcher, teacher, scientist informed of latest publications appearing in their restricted fields of research of the periodical intervals. It is achieved by preparing document profile/list for the users. CAS can be given in following ways i.e.

(a) Announcement of research in progress;

(b)Notifications of forthcoming seminars / conferences

(c) Routing of periodicals; and

(d) Library bulletins i.e. displaying of new arrivals of books and periodicals.

Selective dissemination of information

SDI was originally a phrase related to library and information science. SDI refers to tools and resources used to keep a user informed of new resources on specified topics.SDI services pre-date the world wide web, and the term itself is somewhat dated. Contemporary analogous systems for SDI services include alerts, current awareness tools or trackers. These systems provide automated searches that inform the user of the availability of new resources meeting the user's specified keywords and search parameters. Alerts can be received a number of ways, including email, RSS feeds, voice mail, Instant messaging, and text messaging.Selective dissemination of information was a concept first described by Hans Peter Luhn of IBM in the 1950s. Software was developed in many companies and in government to provide this service in the 1950s and 60s, which allowed distribution of items recently published in abstract journals to be routed to individuals who are likely to be interested in the contents. For example, the system at Ft. Monmouth automatically sent out (by mail) a different set of abstracts to each of about 1,000 scientists and engineers in the army depending on what they were working on. The selection was based on an "interest profile," a list of keywords that described their interests. In some organizations, the 'interest profile' was much more than a simple list of keywords. Librarians or information professionals conducted extensive interviews with their clients to establish a fairly complex profile for each individual. Based on these profiles, the information professionals would then distribute selectively appropriate information to their clients. This labour-intensive operation, while initially costly, over time was made less so. A survey at the time (1970s) indicated that a large number of projects were affected by the SDI service. The software was developed by Edward Housman at the Signal Corps Research Laboratories Technical Information Division.

Reference service

Reference service is the supreme and ultimate function of the library. This is infect the hub of all library activities. Reference service is sometimes referred to as 'reference and information services' or 'reader services'. According to A.B. Kroeger – Reference service as "assistance in the use of resources of the library"..According to James I. Wyer – "Reference service is that part of library administration which deals with the assistance given to the readers in their use of the resources of the library."According to Margaret Hutchins– "Reference service includes the direct, personal aid within a library to persons in search of information for whatever purpose and also various library activities specially aimed at making information as easily available as possible."

Functions of reference service:

The functions of reference service are:

1. **Supervision function:** This function consist of,

- Proper organization of facilities;
- Selection of reference materials;
- Direction of personnel, and
- Study of the library clientele.

2. **The information function:** The reference librarian should be prepared to answer all types of questions and should be able to produce source that would answer the questions. Attempts have also been made to classify questions in various ways. Reference librarian should be prepared to give assistance to the enquirer as much as he requires.

3. **The guidance function:** The reference librarian should be able to give guidance to the readers in the choice of books and other reading materials and should guide them in the location of documents.

4. **The instruction function:** A reference Librarian should instruct the readers about how to work in the library, the use of catalogue and reference works, the location of materials, etc. For this an orientation programmed should be arranged to familiarize the readers with the library practices and procedures.

5. **The bibliographic function:** The bibliographies in various subjects of interest to the readers, should be prepared by the reference staff, so that

the readers are able to know the books and other reading materials in a particular subject.

6. **The appraisal function:** The success in reference service largely depends upon two factors:
7. i) Possession of right material.
8. ii) Knowledge of how to get the most out of it

Referral Service

Whenever the information required by the library user is either not available in the library or is not within the subject expertise of a particular library, then the users are usually directed to sources outside the library, where they would find the required information. Outside source may be a person and/or an organization or an agency. Such service is called referral service. Referral service does not provide users with the document or information needed by them, but directs them to sources of information where required document or information would be available.

Online Dictionary of Library and Information Science defines referral service as 'A type of reference transaction in which patrons with an information need are directed to a reputable person or agency outside the library.'

The referral service is also known as 'information and referral service (I&R)'. The Online Dictionary of Library and Information Science defines this service as "A service available at no charge, usually from a public library or public service agency, providing contact information about other organizations, and individuals qualified to offer specific information and services, both free and fee based, usually within the local community." Another definition of I&R by Robert Croneberger and Carolyn Luck is "The active process of linking a person with a need or problem with a service which will meet the need and solve the problem". This type of service provides detailed information, including contact information, mailing address where a person can go and receive the required help.

DOCUMENT DELIVERY SERVICE (DDS)

The document delivery service also known as document supply service, is concerned with the supply of document, either original or its copy, in print or in electronic form, to the user on demand.

Online Dictionary of Library and Information Science defines DDS as "Provision of published or unpublished documents in hardcopy, microform, or digital format, usually, for a fixed fee upon request."

The DDS is culminating point of all access services. Most of the other information services like CAS, Indexing and abstracting services, literature search services, etc. inform the users about currently published sources of information in their area of interest, whereas DDS actually locates the original document and supplies it to the user. DDS is one of the most important services, as value and importance of other services is directly dependent upon efficiency of this service. For example, if a user alerted by a current awareness service, requires an original document listed in the service and efforts are not made to procure and supply the document to the user in time, the CAS will have no value for him. The DDS thus, adds value to other information services.

Literature search Service

As part of your project or dissertation, you will need to undertake a literature search. This is a search designed to identify existing research and information about your chosen topic. From the materials you find you will produce a literature review. This is a written piece summarizing and analyzing the literature you have found through your search.

Literature search service is a systematic and well-organized search from the already published data to identify a breadth of good quality references on a specific topic .The reasons for conducting literature search are numerous that include drawing information for making evidence-based guidelines, a step in the research

Using the published literature is a core part of the academic communication process. It connects your work to wider scholarly knowledge, demonstrates your understanding, and puts any research you have done in a wider context.

You need to use the published literature in order to:

• provide an academic basis to your research

• clarify your ideas and findings

• find data and research methods

• identify potential issues with the work you plan to do

Some projects involve conducting your own studies, in others you may be analysing the literature itself, or other primary sources. In all these cases, the information you find in your literature search should inform and underpin everything you do, including the methods you use and your discussion of your findings.

Riverview of Literature Search service

Literature review or **narrative review** is a type of review article. A literature review is a scholarly paper, which includes the current knowledge including substantive findings, as well as theoretical and methodological contributions to a particular topic. Literature reviews are secondary sources, and do not report new or original experimental work. Most often associated with academic-oriented literature, such reviews are found in academic journals, and are not to be confused with book reviews that may also appear in the same publication. Literature reviews are a basis for research in nearly every academic field.

A narrow-scope literature review may be included as part of a peer-reviewed journal article presenting new research, serving to situate the current study within the body of the relevant literature and to provide context for the reader. In such a case, the review usually precedes the methodology and results sections of the work.

Producing a literature review may also be part of graduate and post-graduate student work, including in the preparation of a thesis, dissertation, or a journal article. Literature reviews are also common in a research proposal or prospectus (the document that is approved before a student formally begins a dissertation or thesis)

REPROGRAPHICAL SERVICES

T.P Saxsena writes that reprography 'signifies all the various activities and techniques associated with facsimile reproduction of documents, microfilms, microprint, Photostat, reflex copy, xerography, thermo-fax, diazo, offset and all other bewildering varieties of process used for making copies of documents constitute reprography. Reprography thus meant copying and preparation of one or more copies of a document can be reproduced rapidly and economically through reprographic methods. It is thus applied widely in processing the information be making copies of published, unpublished material, rare documents, manuscripts, pages of periodicals, books, Newspapers, graphic material etc.

BIBLIOGRAPHIC SERVICES

The Oxford English Dictionary defines" Bibliography, as "A list of books of a particular author, Publisher or country, or of those dealing with any particular theme; the literature of a subject. In other words a bibliography is, " A list of written, printed or otherwise produced records of civilization., which may include books, serials, pictures, maps, films, recordings, museum objects, manuscripts and any other media of the communication.(Shores).

LITERATURE SEARCHES ON DEMAND

Some of the IRI's conducts surveys on literature interest to faculty members/ Research scholars and compiles bibliographies in response to reference queries by the scholars on demand. These bibliographies are published from time to time, name a few as:- Similarly they also prepare abstracts of the reference and also provide photocopies of their full versions.

ABSTRACTING SERVICES

Abstract acts as retrieval media and current awareness tool. According to Allen Kent "An abstract is a summary of a publication or an article accompanied by an adequate bibliographical description to enable the publication or article to be traced. Robert L. Collinson writes that an abstract is the "terse presentation in the author's own language, of all the points made in the same order as in the original piece of primary documentary information - that can be a book, a research report, a periodical article, speech, the proceeding of the conference, an interview, etc

In nutshell an Abstract is an abbreviated, accurate representation of the basic characteristics of the original. In many cases Abstracts function as surrogates for the original document. Its purpose is to draw attention to the information contained in the original document and provide whether or not to refer to original. The Abstracts are frequently arranged in classified order

INDEXING SERVICES

The word index is derived from the Latin word 'indicate' which means to indicate or point out. ' An index is a tool by means of which a person who needs information has it indicated or pointed out him. Allen Kent defined index "As a device that serves as a pointer or indicator, most often alphabetic lists that includes subjects and name of people or places that are considered to be special pertinence in a graphic records.1 Similarly, Geogre S. Bonn writes that an index is a detailed alphabetical list of names, terms, topics, places, formulae, numbers, or other significant terms in a completed work with exact page reference to material discussed in that work/ Thus, an index is a systematically arranged list giving enough information about each item to enable it to be a link between a specific subject or topic and the identified document

TRANSLATION SERVICES

It is observed that 40% of the world's output of Ideological literature is in languages other than English, the Indologist must therefore, have access to such literature pertaining to their specialized fields. Towards meeting this need, some of the IRIs has organized its translation section backed by its team of well qualified and experienced translators, who can translate Ideological material from languages like Chinese, German, French, Japanese and Russian and some other Indian Languages i.e. Tamil, Malyalam, Hindi, Sanskrit. The type of documents translated includes Journals, articles, Reports and books. In some cases the translation is done "Cover to Cover" and in other cases only abstracts of the documents are made in English. To meet the demands of Ideologists, some IRI's have started the following activities in this respect

1. Praci-Joyti; digest of TNDOLOGY by ISIS,KUK.

2. LMIS (Library Management and Information System) by IGNCA, New Delhi

3. Sahitya Akadmi, New Delhi.

Chapter 7
Library Automation

INTRODUCTION

The word 'Automation' has been derived from a Greek word 'Automate' which means something which has the power of spontaneous motion or self-movement (Webster's Third New International Dictionary of English Language, 1966). The term 'Automation' was first introduced by D.S. Harder in 1936, who was then with the General Motor Company in the United States. He used the term automation to mean automatic handling of parts between progressive production processes.

However, the modern usage of the word "automation" is not in vogue in the above sense.

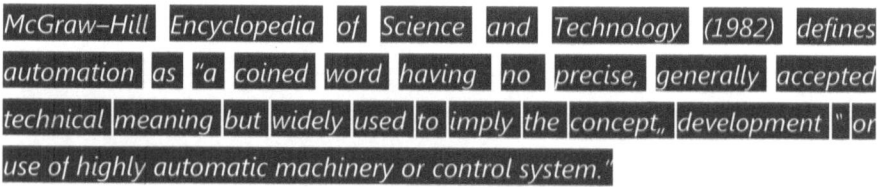

McGraw–Hill Encyclopedia of Science and Technology (1982) defines automation as "a coined word having no precise, generally accepted technical meaning but widely used to imply the concept,, development " or use of highly automatic machinery or control system.'

From the above definition, one can observe that 'automation' is the application of 'machines' to perform a task automatically.

The word 'library automation' is being used in literature for the last four decades. A perusal of the literature would indicate that many authors have not tried to define the term explicitly. They use the term 'Library automation' to mean the use of computers as an aid for library activities. However, some authors have tried to define the term. For instance Markers on (1967) says "Library automation in the broadest sense can be taken to mean the employment of machines for library processes. In general, however, library automation has come to mean the application of computers and related data processing equipment to libraries.

Salmon (1975), has tried to give a more exhaustive definition. According to him "Library automation is the use of automatic and semi-automatic library activities as acquisition, cataloguing, and circulation. Although these activities are not necessarily performed in 90 traditionally associated with libraries; library automation may thus be distinguished from related fields such as information retrieval, automatic indexing and abstracting, and automatic textual analysis."

Further, he says that "linguistic purists have argued rightly that the term 'automation' applies more correctly and narrowly to automatic process control... and 'library automation' is now far the most commonly used term for mechanisation of library activities using data processing equipment."

Form the first part of the above definition it can be observed that the term 'library automation' is used to imply just the mechanization of traditional and/or manual house–keeping routines of a library. In other words, it confines itself to the use of data processing equipment and associated technology to perform exactly what has always and already been done in libraries through a manual process, of course, with the justification of reduced cost and/or increased performance. However, literature shows that such distinction is not maintained. The scope of library automation goes beyond the automation of just house–keeping activities of the libraries.

Hayes and Becker (1970) have identified the area of library automation. According to them, the areas of library automation include:

1. The application of data processing equipment to do/to support the clerical/repetitive functions found in technical processing circulation control and serials control.
2. The application of data processing equipment to the fields of information storage and retrieval, automatic indexing and abstracting and in reference work; and
3. The application of computers/data processing equipment for operation research and system analysis.

It is observed that much work has been done in the first two areas, where as one finds les literature on the third. Though it might be difficult to find a universally accepted and a comprehensive definition of library automation, one can accept the areas identified by Hayes and Becker as coming under the purview of library automation. Library automation offers many opportunities to improve service to library patrons.

Among other benefits, it makes materials easier for patrons to Locate as well as allowing staff to better serve patrons by facilitating a Multitude of staff tasks such as acquisitions, cataloguing, circulation and Reference. On the other hand, the financial and staff commitment needed to Move to an automated system or from one system to another is substantial And long-lasting. Automation cannot be approached as a panacea for Systemic problems in a library. Without staff support and training, no system Can offer its full potential.

Your strategic vision must now provide the framework or context for the next step in the automation Process, which is to determine which library functions, should be automated and in what order of priority. For example, processes that are repetitive occupy large amounts of staff time, require retrieving Information from large, unwieldy files, or are high-profile functions of the library (such as the public catalog) are prime candidates for automation.

Determining the functions that you wish to automate and their priorities relative to each other is important for all sorts of reasons. If needs and priorities are clear, functions can be automated in phases, allowing for more effective use of frequently scarce funding. Moreover, it is a way to develop credibility with funding agencies and be able to take advantage of "sudden" funding opportunities. Finally, evaluations of systems and options will be easier and more productive if you are able to match your highest functional priorities against the corresponding modules available in the marketplace.

Basic Components of Library automation:

The followings are the basic components of library Automation..

1. Computer System.
2. Networking Device.
3. Software.

4. Database.
5. Server.

1. Computer:

A computer is an electronic device that has the ability to accept data, store data, and automatically execute an instruction, to perform mathematical, logical or manipulative operation to produce output. A computer system consists of a number of individual components performing a particular function.

A computer system has input, output, storage's and processing components as the basic elements. Some of them are as:

2. Input device:

A device that can be used to insert data into a computer or other computational device is known as input device. Some of common input devices are:

3Keyboard:

It looks like a key board of a type writer that enables us to enter data into a computer. Keyboard is the most popular and commonly used input device.

3Mouse:

In computing, a mouse is a pointing device. It looks like a small plastic box with two buttons and a scroll wheel and connected by cable with computer.

4. Optical Character Reader (OCR):

A method of reading character that have been printed or typed in a special type front. By means of a photo electric scanner device, which converts the light patterns into digital signal for computer.

5. Optical Mark Reader (OMR):

A special scanning device that can read carefully placed pencil marks on specially designed documents, like form , answer sheets, etc.

6. Bar-code Reader:

A bar-code reader is an electronic device for reading printed barcodes on paper by the help of computer. This is very helpful device for a librarian to find out the basic information of a book.

7. Scanner:
Scanner allows a PC to connect a drawing or photograph into digital format. This device is helpful to build-up a automated library collection.

8.Voice Data Entry:
Voice or speech data entry system, that accepts the spoken word as input data or commands via a microphone.

9Output device:

An output device is any peripheral device that converts machine readable information into people readable form. Some commonly used output devices are:

10. Monitor:
The monitor is the commonly used display device. It output signal as image format or display. It is vary useful device for automated library system.

11. Printer:
A printer is an output device that produces a hard copy of data or paper sheet. we can prepared / print catalogue card or bibliography by using printer.

12. Central Processing Unit:
The main part of a computer in which operations are controlled and executed. It contains most important hardware of a computer. It also called the brain of a computer.

13. Storage / Memory:
A computer system contains a variety of memory devices to store instruction and data for its operation. This mainly two types:
1. Primary Memory, e.g. RAM, ROM etc.
2. Secondary memory, e.g. Magnetic disk, Hard-desk, Floppy disk etc.

This devices are very important for automated library system, because you can store books, journals and documents in digital format on storage device.

2. Networking Device: Networking device includes the following devices:

- **Modem:** An electronic communication system that allow two or more inter connected computers and terminals to share information and resources.
- **LAN:** A Local Area Network is a data communication network used to interconnect data terminal equipment distributed over a limited area (typically up-to 10 square km.).
- **MAN:** A Metropolitan Area Network is a computer network that usually spans a city or a large campus. A MAN usually interconnects a number of Local Area Network.
- **WAN:** A Wide Area Network connects computers located across a wide geographical area e.g. Internet is best known as WAN. Telecommunication links might involves common cities, microwave of satellite communication.
- **Cable:** Networking cables are used to connect one networking device to another networking devices or to connect two or more computers to share printer, scanner etc.

3. Software: Software is a collection of computer programs and related data that provides the instruction for telling a computer what to do and how to do it. To build-up an automated library collection, use of computer software is very important. Without using library software we cannot build-up an automated library collection.

Some of the popular automated library software are:

- Koha,
- OpenBiblio,
- Evergreen,
- Green Stone Library Software, etc.

4. Database: A database is an integrated collection of logically related records or objects. Database is very essential for an automated library system, because all the basic information of books are stored on database. It may be as Author database, Bibliographic Database, etc.

6. **Server:** A computer or computer program that manages or controls the access to centralized resource or service in a network.

By using server you can share your library e-resources with other libraries who are connected with the server.

Conclusion:

The motto of Library Automation is to provide the right information, to right person, in right manner, in right time. While justifying need of library automation more than cost-effectiveness the benefits derived by the library users become the major consideration. Since library does not happen to be an economic entry such benefits need to be looked at in a different perspective. To appreciate the advantages it becomes necessary to highlight the different levels of library automation.

Chapter 8

APPLICATION OF ICT IN LIBRARY

INTRODUCTION

Information has emerged as the prime in the 21st century. ICT has exerted a profound influence on traditional academic libraries. They have no option but adapt themselves to new developments, especially due to cuts in budget allocation. Hence, networking of information centers is inevitable. The prime objectives of the library is pooling information resources and information related infrastructure and sharing them. In this process, many library have reexamined their traditional methods and services to overcome inadequacies trough automation and computerization. The use of computers for library operation avoids respectively jobs and saves considerable amount of time, resources and labor. It also speeds up technical processing and information services. ICT has been a means to bring quality services. Systematic planning of its introduction and application will assure that the technology based information services are sustainable, and enhances the ability of library. In the present scenario, the library and information centers at global level are able to provide access to;

• Online databases across the country and worldwide

• Comprehensive statistical databases and content page services

• Full text information sources with key word searching

CONCEPT OF INFORMATION COMMUNICATION TECHNOLOGY (ICT)

The term Information and Communication Technology (ICT) is more commonly used. Whilst Information Technology (IT) has been the accepted term in the UK and USA, it is not the universal term. Telemetric is widely used in France, and Information is also used elsewhere in this sense. ICT deals with the use of electronic computer and computer software to convert, store, protect, process, transmit, and retrieve information.

NEEEDS OF INFORMATION TECHNOLOGY

Due to information explosion it is very difficult to handle large information with traditional library tools like manual catalogue, bibliographies, etc. In today's library environment, to provide the right way, is not possible without ICT application. ICT has become necessity and need. 4. IMPACT OF INFORMATION COMMUNICATION TECHNOLOGY In old days library was considered as mere storehouse of knowledge. But these days ICT has reshaped the functioning and services of libraries. The activities which were carried out manually are being carried out effectively and smoothly with the help of ICT. ICT has changed the way of acquisition, technical processing, periodical subscription, and circulation activities etc. in such a way that library readers can get desired information and services effectively in shortest time with less man power involvement. This is the information age because information technology is growing fast. Traditional libraries are changing their role and functions according to the new trends in the society. Library is providing information through the computers and internet. It can be said that without the help of the computers and internet any library information Centre cannot satisfy the users.

NECESSITY FOR ICT IN LIBRARIES

To speed-up accurate and reliable data transfer in future there is also a danger of non-availability of hard copies of documents, particularly to secondary sources that are available only on CDROM. Knowing this, continuing education about ICT for libraries is essential. Due to the escalation in prices of periodicals and books, no library can afford to acquire all the publications; resource sharing through networking is the only option. To participate in the network, computerization of libraries is a prerequisite. Many International databases like DIALOG, MEDLARS, INIS, AGRIS, etc. are delivering the information electronically. Unless the libraries are automated, there is no possibility for accessing the information from these global level databases. The literature in almost all the fields is increasing tremendously and in a multidimensional way. Because of this growth, manual bibliographic control is not feasible and ICT is needed. The information seeking behaviour of the users is also changing according to their varied needs. To meet these hanging needs, storage capacities of information and retrieval techniques should be improved. The quality, user friendless, effectiveness, reliability and regularity of library services can be much improved through ICT.

1) To utilize the growing world of electronic information, application of ICT is necessary.

2) With the help of ICT it is possible to gain local, national, regional and international reputation.

3) To be able to provide round the clock access and service to users.

4) To access experienced and expert individuals in my fields;

5) To provide regular updates on topics of interest to users;

6) To promote teamwork across geographical distance

ICT-BASED USER SERVICES

Some library users are adopting electronic habits, making increasing use of the new ICT including computers, the Internet, the Web, Intranet, Extranet and other technologies. As a result, library users are placing new demands on their libraries. They require access to the latest information, updated information resources and access to ICT facilities that they could use in their work. Use of ICT in libraries enhances user's satisfaction. It provides numerous benefits to library users. Some of the benefits are:

• Provide speedy and easy access to information

• Provides remote access to users

• Provides round the clock access to users

• Provides access to unlimited information from different sources

• Provides information flexibility to be used by any individual according to his/her requirements

• Provides increased flexibility

• Facilitates the reformatting and combining of data from different sources

Libraries are also providing various ICT-based services to their user, including the following Provision of Web access to OPACs

• Electronic document delivery

• Networked information resources

• Delivery of information to user desktops

• Online instructions• Online readers advisory services

ADVANTAGES OF USING ICT IN THE LIBRARY

The advantages of ICT are:

• ICT makes library work easier, faster, cheaper and more effective.

• Helps to manage information overload as information retrieval is made easier in

• computerized systems. Remote access is enabled through networked systems

• Computerization saves space and reduces paper.

CHALLENGES OF USING ICT IN LIBRARIES

The challenges of ICT are:

•Poor funding of ICT infrastructures

• Constant change of software and hardware

• Erratic power supply• Insufficient bandwidth

• Lack of technical IT knowledge by library staff

• Copyright and intellectual property rights management•

CONCLUSION

In fact, it is now difficult to imagine a world without information technology. The provision and use of ICT is part and parcel of the entire system, to both the students, information professionals and the institutions. With the help of ICT to deliver the services of their user is very easy and fast and also it can save the time of user and staff both. Nowadays ICT has totally changed the concept of library and information center as it was in early days. Libraries are adopting ICT for performing both housekeeping operations as well as for providing services to the library patrons. Application of ICT has added value to the services and libraries are becoming popular among the patrons. With the aid of ICT libraries are actually marching towards achieving the goal of providing pinpointed exhaustive and expeditious information to those who are in need of that information. Information and communication technology is applied for providing information services which are more convenient, better accessible and cost effective.

Reference:

1. https://en.wikipedia.org/wiki/Library((*Accessed on 23rd August 2017)*)

2. KRISHAN KUMAR. Theory of classification. 1993. Vikas Publishing; New Delhi.

3. Kishan Kumar (1993). Cataloguing. New Delhi: Har-Anand.Kishan Kumar

4. Khan (TM), Information Organization and Communication, New Delhi, Ess E ss,1998. 6- Khanna (J.K), Library and society Ed.2.-New Delhi: EssEss Publications, 1994.

5. Girija Kumar and Krishan Kumar. Theory Cataloguing Ed 5, Delhi Vikas 1986.

6. M ukherjee, A.K. Reference W work and its Tools. 3rd rev. ed. Calcutta: W world Press, 1975. 8- Ranganathan (SR) Reference Service ed.2. Bombay, Asia. 1961

7. Khanna, J.K.. Documentation and Inform action Services, System s and Technique. Agra: Y.K. Publishers, 2000.